Thank you for your purchase!

This book was made to brighten your day - Have fun!

Please leave us a review @ Amazon

• • • • • • • ❖ • • • • • • •

Happy Coloring!

`D1561023`

Theo's Bellini

Ingredients:
2 ounces peach puree
4 ounces chilled prosecco
Peach slice, for garnish

Instructions:
1. Gather the ingredients.
2. Pour a measurement of peach puree into each Champagne flute.
3. Slowly top with sparkling wine while gently stirring to incorporate. If you like, garnish with a slice of peach, either slit and rested on the rim or dropped into the glass.

Bailey's Coconut Colada

Ingredients:

2 ounces Banks 5-Island rum
1 ounce pineapple juice, freshly squeezed
1/2 ounce lime juice, freshly squeezed
1 scoop coconut sorbetto such as Ciao Bella or Häagen-Dazs
Garnish: dried coconut flakes

Instructions:

1. Add the Banks 5-Island rum, pineapple juice, lime juice and coconut sorbet to a shaker with ice and shake until well-chilled.
2. Double-strain into a chilled rocks or coupe glass or a coconut shell.
3. Garnish with dried coconut flakes and pineapple.

Hank's Manhattan

Ingredients:

2 ounces rye whiskey
1 ounce sweet vermouth
2 dashes Angostura bitters
1 dash orange bitters
Garnish: brandied cherry or lemon twist

Instructions:

1. Add the bourbon (or rye), sweet vermouth and both bitters to a mixing glass with ice, and stir until well-chilled.
2. Strain into a chilled coupe.
3. Garnish with a brandied cherry or a lemon twist.

Sandra's Blue Lagoon

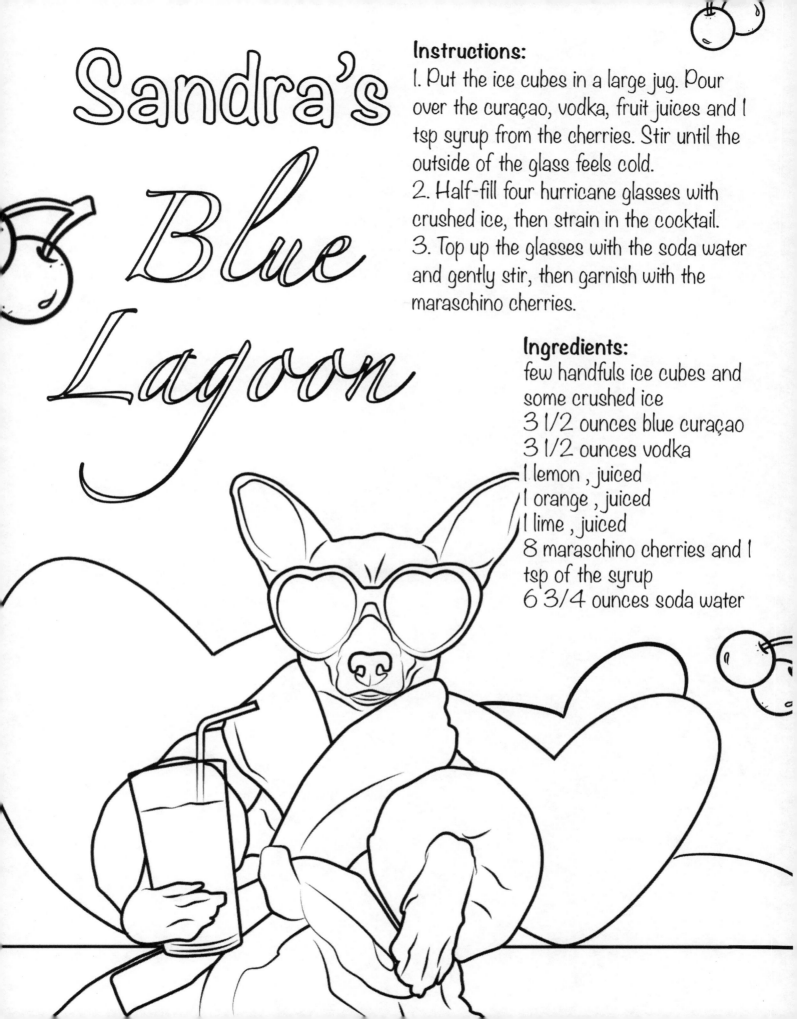

Instructions:
1. Put the ice cubes in a large jug. Pour over the curaçao, vodka, fruit juices and 1 tsp syrup from the cherries. Stir until the outside of the glass feels cold.
2. Half-fill four hurricane glasses with crushed ice, then strain in the cocktail.
3. Top up the glasses with the soda water and gently stir, then garnish with the maraschino cherries.

Ingredients:
few handfuls ice cubes and some crushed ice
3 1/2 ounces blue curaçao
3 1/2 ounces vodka
1 lemon , juiced
1 orange , juiced
1 lime , juiced
8 maraschino cherries and 1 tsp of the syrup
6 3/4 ounces soda water

Charlie's Martini

Ingredients:

2 ounces dry gin

1 ounce dry vermouth

1 dash orange bitters (optional, but highly recommended)

Instructions:

1. Combine ingredients in a mixing glass and fill with ice.

2. Stir well to chill and strain into a chilled cocktail glass.

3. Twist a piece of lemon peel over the drink and use as garnish, or, if you must, toss in an olive.

Penny's
Piña Colada

Instructions:

Blend: Place the white rum, coconut cream, pineapple juice and chunks, and ice in a blender. Process until totally blended.

Pour: Pour into glasses and top with and top with the golden rum (it should float on top).

Serve: Serve with pineapple leaves or slices as garnish if desired.

Ingredients:

6 ounces white rum
6 ounces cream of coconut
6 ounces pineapple juice
1/2 cup frozen pineapple chunks
(see How to Cut a Pineapple)
4 cups ice
4 ounces golden or añejo rum
Pineapple leaves or wedges for garnish, optional

Rocky's Long Island Iced Tea

Ingredients:
½ fluid ounce vodka
½ fluid ounce rum
½ fluid ounce gin
½ fluid ounce tequila
½ fluid ounce triple sec (orange-flavored liqueur)
1 fluid ounce sweet and sour mix
1 fluid ounce cola, or to taste
1 lemon slice

Instructions:
1. Fill a cocktail shaker with ice.
2. Pour vodka, rum, gin, tequila, triple sec, and sour mix over ice; cover and shake.
3. Pour cocktail into a Collins or hurricane glass; top with splash of cola for color.
4. Garnish with a lemon slice.

Daisy's *Daiquiris*

Instructions:
1. Gather the ingredients.
2. Add the ingredients to a cocktail shaker with ice cubes.
3. Shake well.
4. Strain into a chilled cocktail glass.
5. Serve and enjoy.

Ingredients:

1 1/2 ounces light rum

3/4 ounce freshly squeezed lime juice

1/2 to 3/4 ounce simple syrup, to taste

Cassandra's Cosmopolitan

Ingredients:
30 ml Cointreau L'Unique
60 ml Vodka
30 ml Cranberry juice
30 ml Fresh lime juice

Instructions:
1. Combine all ingredients in a cocktail shaker
2. Add ice and shake until well-chilled
3. Strain into a chilled coupe or cocktail glass
4. Garnish with an orange twist

Frank & Hal's
Fruit Cocktail

Ingredients:

1 1/2 cups pineapple juice

1 cup apple juice

1/2 cup orange juice

1 tbsp. freshly squeezed lemon juice

1 pear core removed and sliced

3 oz rum divided (optional)

Instructions:

1. Combine all the ingredients (except rum if omitting,) into a mixing bowl or pitcher. Chill in refrigerator until ready to serve.

2. Pour over ice in tall glasses and garnish with additional pear and lemon slices.

3. Note: You can add 1 1/2 oz of rum into each glass before serving if you want to save some of the beverage as alcohol-free.

Lucy's Pink Lady

Ingredients:
1 1/2 ounces gin
1/2 ounce applejack
1/2 ounce freshly squeezed lemon juice
1/2 ounce grenadine
1 small egg white
Maraschino cherry, for garnish

Instructions:
1. Gather the ingredients.
2. In a cocktail shaker filled with ice cubes, pour the gin, applejack, lemon juice, and grenadine, and measure out 1/4 to 1/2 ounce of the egg white.
3. Shake vigorously for at least 30 seconds.
4. Strain into a chilled cocktail glass. Garnish with a cherry.

Eddie's Espresso Martini

Ingredients:
2 ounces vodka
1/2 ounce coffee liqueur usually
Kahlúa
1 ounce espresso freshly brewed
(or cold brew concentrate)
1/2 ounce simple syrup
Garnish: coffee beans

Instructions:
1. Brew the coffee and let it cool completely.
2. Add ice to a cocktail shaker then add the cooled coffee, simple syrup, kahlua and vodka.
3. Shake very hard so the foam is formed then strain it quickly into a martini glass. Top with coffee beans, serve.

Duke's Pineapple Daiquiri

Instructions:

1. Combine all ingredients into cocktail shaker and shake to chill and dilute the mixture.
2. Strain into coupe glass.

Ingredients:

2 ounces white rum
½ ounce pineapple juice
1 ounce lime juice
½ ounce simple syrup

Archie's
Whiskey Sour

Ingredients:
1 1/2 ounces bourbon
1 ounce lemon juice
1/2 ounce 2:1 sugar syrup
2 dashes Angostura bitters
½ fresh egg white
ice
50p-sized piece of lemon zest
slice of orange and a cherry on
a stick for garnish

Instructions:
1. Shake all of the
ingredients (except for
the lemon zest) hard with
ice and strain into an
ice-filled rocks glass.
2. Squeeze the lemon
zest, shiny side down
over the drink so the
scented oils spray
across the surface.
Discard the zest, add the
garnish and serve.

Max's MOJITO

Ingredients:

10 fresh mint leaves
½ medium lime, cut into 3 wedges, divided
2 tablespoons white sugar, or to taste
1 cup ice cubes, or as needed
1½ fluid ounces white rum
½ cup club soda, or as needed

Instructions:

1. Place mint leaves and 1 lime wedge into a sturdy glass. Use a muddler and crush to release mint oils and lime juice.

2. Add remaining lime wedges and 2 tablespoons sugar, and muddle again to release the lime juice. Do not strain the mixture.

3. Fill the glass almost to the top with ice. Pour in rum and fill the glass with club soda.
4. Stir, taste, and add more sugar if desired.

Ben and Jo's Margarita

Instructions:

1. Rub the rim of the glass with the lime slice to make the salt stick to it. Shake the other ingredients with ice, then carefully pour into the glass (taking care not to dislodge any salt).

2. Garnish and serve over ice.

Ingredients:

1 oz Orange Liqueur

1 oz Lime juice

2 oz Silver Tequila